FOUNDING A SCHOOL IN FRANCE: L'ECOLE HAMPSHIRE

Text and Watercolours
by
Jane Box-Grainger

A Sequel to *A Vision Achieved*
by
David Lemmon

For Tom

with very best wishes

Jan Box-Grainger 2008.

ARTHUR H. STOCKWELL LTD
Torrs Park   Ilfracombe   Devon
Established 1898
www.ahstockwell.co.uk

British Library Cataloguing-in-Publication Data.
A catalogue record for this book is available
from the British Library.

Arthur H. Stockwell Ltd bears no responsibility
for the accuracy of information recorded in this book.

Every effort has been made to obtain the necessary permission with
reference to copyright material, both illustrative and quoted. We
apologise for any omissions in this respect and will be pleased to
make the appropriate acknowledgements in any future edition.

Dedication:
To my children, Eve, Paul and Jill, and to
my sisters and brother, Ann, Susan and John.

ISBN 978-0-7223-4023-3
Printed in Great Britain by
Arthur H. Stockwell Ltd
Torrs Park   Ilfracombe
Devon

Contents

Index of Watercolours

Glossary

Bastide	Fortified town
Bloc en calcaire	Made of limestone
Borie	Ancient Shepherd's hut
Bulletin de paie	Payslip
Bureau de Beaux Arts	Group overseeing and protecting historical buildings
Chemin rural	Lane
Commune	Group (in this case, villagers)
Commune land	Land owned by the village
Conseils	Equivalent of local councillors
Contrat de durée limitée	Contract of employment with starting and ending dates
Convention	Agreement in writing
Cour	Courtyard
Crépissage	Roughcast covering original stone
Direction Générale des Impôts	Tax authority
Domaine	Estate
Ecole primaire	Primary school
Femme de ménage	Housekeeper
Four	Oven (bakehouse oven)
Gabare	Flat-bottomed boat on the Dordogne
Gérant	Managing director of a company
Grange	Barn
Hôtels-des-particuliers	Private mansions (Sarlat)
La France Profonde	Remote French countryside
Lauzes	Crafted limestone tiles
Maire	Mayor
Mairie	Mayor's office
Maître d'oeuvres	Foreman of works

5

Mas	Farmhouse
Notaire	Solicitor
Pierres jaunes	Yellow limestone bricks
Pigeonnier	Pigeon loft
Place	Square (village square)
Pompe Oxyfor	Sewage pump
Porcherie	Pigsty
Poste	Post for electricity or phone wires
Poutres	Roof beams
Remparts	Town/city walls
Rez-de-chaussée	Ground floor
SA	Public company
Salle de classe	Classroom
Salle des fêtes	Village hall
Salon	Sitting room
Sarl	Limited company
Squelettes	Skeletons
Sud Ouest	Local newspaper
Trimestral	Quarterly
Tuiles plats brunes	Flat brown tiles
TVA	VAT

Chapter 1

Founding a School in France

This chronicle is the story of an educational project from its conception to its successful conclusion. It was to prepare pupils to take their place eventually in the newly formed European Union by giving them greater exposure to a foreign language than the curriculum would normally allow. The language selected was French because the pupils already had a grounding in French in their London school, The Hampshire School, Knightsbridge, a well-respected and successful preparatory operation. In order to create a sister school in France, it was essential to find some suitable premises as its base. The search to find a suitable and practical venue in France is the first stage of this story. The second stage was to turn the selected Grade II listed buildings into an attractive and practical site. The final stage was to implement the syllabus. All these stages were time-consuming, and, in some cases, costly. It is extremely gratifying to me as the instigator and author of this book that they have finally proved to be successful. I still find it amazing that what, at times appeared to be insurmountable difficulties were overcome, and that the project succeeded.

If I reveal a few brief details about the history of The

Hampshire School in Knightsbridge, it may help the reader both to enjoy and understand this story.

The founder, my mother, June Hampshire, started a school in the drawing room of her home in Surrey in 1928, to teach dancing. June suffered from post-natal depression after the birth of her second daughter, Ann. June's doctor asked her what she would like to do. Her reply was "Dance!" She had been a ballet dancer before her marriage, so it seemed logical to use the large drawing room in Oakgates, her house in Surrey, as a starting point for teaching a few pupils. The room had parquet flooring and enough space once the furniture had been pushed to the sides of the room. It was called the Jane Ann School of Dancing after her two eldest daughters, Jane and Ann. She taught ballroom, tap, ballet and general dancing. It was so successful that many pupils joined the classes and she had to rent two extra spaces, Cheam Hall and the ballroom of the Drift Bridge Hotel in Epsom. Then later, in 1935, she also opened an attractive studio in Epsom High Street. Throughout the period from 1928 to 1939, June's pupils gave regular concerts and recitals to help to raise money for local worthy causes. Jane and Ann were a regular feature in the concerts, where they danced special 'duets' choreographed by their mother. In 1932, June rented a studio in Knightsbridge, the London Ballet School, while in Surrey the school continued under its original name. With the opening of the London Ballet School, June expanded the curriculum to include tuition on elocution, music and dramatic art. The new curriculum also included courses in shorthand, typing and French for senior pupils, as well as professional training for the stage. All activities stopped in both schools in 1939, due to the commencement of World War II.

On June's return to London, after three years serving in the WRAAF, the school in Knightsbridge reopened. It incorporated general education with dancing, and June's youngest daughter, Susan, became one of the first six pupils.

In 1943, a flying bomb fell in a field adjoining Oakgates. The blast blew out most of the windows and doors. As no one was living in the house it provided a field day for looters, who practically emptied the house of all its contents. My father, June's husband, was very tardy in taking action and so he sold the lovely property very cheaply – what a pity! So from that time there was no longer a school in Surrey owned by my mother.

In the late 1960s I went back to look at the school's origins in Oakgates, and was devastated to see that the back garden had been sold, and another house had been built on it. In fact, most of the surrounding fields and some of the large gardens had also been used for building.

The London Ballet School was now called Mrs Hampshire's School. Mrs Hampshire's School was concerned mainly with junior pupils. Their curriculum gave them a sound basis on which to build academic success, coupled with training in dance and, in some cases, stage experience, because it included educating her daughter Susan.

This new school was an immediate success and its pupil roll expanded rapidly. This was in part due to June's daughters, Jane and Ann, who were student teachers under their mother's inspired leadership, and the very original and happy ambience they created. The pupil roll continued to increase rapidly, and the school outgrew the space available. This was solved by renting a local church hall, St Saviour's Hall in Walton Place. This new development caused yet another change of name. It was now registered as The Hampshire School with the Ministry of Education. I think it's necessary to clear up some of the confusion which has arisen on occasion. The school was not in the county of Hampshire, but it was named after its founder, June Hampshire. The Hampshire School was now subject to visits from school inspectors. They found the teaching sound and all the pupils happy, so the inspectors overlooked the limited premises. One has to remember that between 1943 and 1948 London was still suffering from the damage and devastation of World War II, and therefore schools were needed – especially if they happened to be operating successfully. The school continued to provide concerts and recitals on a regular basis – now renting West End theatre space in which to perform, i.e. the Adelphi and Fortune theatres. This early start led to a career for a number of well-known dancers and actresses – Lavinia Bertram, Anthony Dowell, Alison Frazer, Michelle Gallagher, Maina Gielgud, Susan Hampshire, Belinda Lang, Linda Marlowe, Josephine Russell and Susan Travis, to name but a few.

In 1948 the lease of Basil Street expired, so from 1949 for the next twenty years the school operated in St Saviour's Hall, despite searches by June for better premises. Nevertheless, the school was a happy, original place; results on the whole were very good, and pupils continued to join.

Chapter 2

New Head and Owner

My mother's decision to retire in 1961 appeared sudden, but at that time she felt tired from all the work connected with the school and successfully bringing up her four children. She had been finding the stress of going to school each day harder and harder to bear, and she was gradually leaving more teaching to be done when she was not there. One has to remember that St Saviour's Hall, with more than fifty pupils in one room, could be very tiring for a sixty-year-old woman. We persuaded her not to retire fully but to continue teaching dancing, which she loved, both in The Hampshire School and in other schools – a much less strenuous programme for her.

June wanted both her daughters to take over the school. Ann had recently married and was now pregnant and was not in a position to take this up as she was looking forward to her family life without the responsibility of a school. I felt I had no choice but to take over the reins, and to continue my mother's work.

I discussed this with my husband, who was enthusiastic about what he considered an opportunity for me in view of the school's good reputation. He promised to help me with the school's secretarial work – for instance, sending out invoices and drafting prospectuses. My husband was a fine wordsmith and almost obsessively correct in written detail! I doubt, with hindsight, if I could have succeeded without his help and cooperation. But he made me make one promise, that the family were not going to live in the school if we eventually succeeded in finding permanent premises for it. I agreed. My husband confirmed that, in many ways I had already taken a large stake in the teaching syllabus, and, with his help, he was sure I would succeed.

There were many facts against my chances of success. First, the school came with no money; secondly, it had no permanent premises despite its enviable reputation; thirdly, I had family commitments with three children under the age of nine years; fourthly, my husband, who had been a fine actor, decided to change his career to give his family the benefit of more regular income; and finally, I had no formal academic qualifications. My career up to that point had been as a member of the corps de ballet with the Anglo-Russian Ballet Company, followed by five years in repertory, starting as an ASM (unpaid), and then progressing to salaried juvenile leads at the Playhouse Theatre, Manchester. As the Genie of the Ring in Aladdin I danced at pantomimes in Southsea and Preston. In between my theatrical work, when I was 'resting', I used to teach in my mother's little school, learning my craft on the hoof, as they say.

What a category for disaster some people thought! Fortunately, due to the loyalty of the parents and staff, who continued to support the school, it was definitely not a disaster – a little unusual, perhaps, but nevertheless a success.

After updating St Saviour's Hall as much as I was permitted, I continued searching for new premises while helping the school, my husband and children. Despite my heavy workload I still found time to search for a permanent home for the school. It took eight long years until, in 1969, I at last found and purchased in my own name a freehold house with school use. It was in Ennismore Gardens, Knightsbridge, London.

Prior to my purchase, Ennismore Gardens had been used in part as a nursery school, while the upper floors were used for the owner to live in. I was fortunate to have John Gray, recommended by Richard Du Cann, QC, who arranged with the planning authorities that I could use the whole building as a school.

The building in Ennismore Gardens needed considerable updating, all of which finally cost nearly £80,000. New RSJs had to support the basement and staircase. A fire escape was constructed from the fourth floor to the ground, and numerous fire doors and toilet facilities were installed. A new small kitchen was constructed in the basement next to the assembly hall, to provide cooked lunches for staff and pupils.

Our friend Alan Fabes, FCA advised me (a) to buy the freehold property in my own name, because I was providing personally the bulk of the money and also taking a personal risk on the repayment of the mortgage; and (b) to found a limited company (that is, a service company) to run the school's financial side. So a company named Hampshire Tutorials Ltd was created in 1969. Alan had recently retired from Cork Gully in the City, and he offered to be bursar for one day a week in order to monitor the limited company. What a successful arrangement that proved to be! Sadly we were unable to use Hampshire School Ltd because that title had already been used by a driving school in Hampshire. Thus Hampshire Tutorials Ltd was selected and the company came into being.

In 1977 Hampshire Tutorials Ltd became the parent company of L'Ecole Hampshire Sarl. Sarl is the French equivalent of a limited company in England. Both companies closed between 2007 and 2008.

Between 1970 and 1974, even with Ennismore Gardens,

the expanding pupil roll demanded even more premises. Sadly, although new suitable premises were found, change of use for a school was denied.

With hindsight I realise I was too trusting and naive about the planning process, and did not push the planners' refusals sufficiently. I was told, on each occasion, that the Foreign Office had plans to use the chosen properties. I was, I'm afraid, too busy to check and devote my time to the planners. If I had, I may have succeeded – or perhaps not, bearing in mind that I had applied for planning permission for residential properties similar to Ennismore Gardens, but with no previous history of school use. I expect that made a difference.

However, a new idea was formulating in my mind, which was to open a sister school in France. The following chapters tell the story of that school.

Chapter 3

Looking for a Suitable Property in France

David Lemmon wrote:

There were, of course, a number of important reasons for looking towards France – not least of which was that integration with Europe was becoming closer every day. The principal European language taught in the School was French, and Miss J... that it was necessary to re-examine the content of the French syllabus and its practice. She was very much aware that low standards of oral French were accepted in many schools and, indeed, by examiners. The statement often expressed – 'Well, everyone speaks English nowadays, so why bother?' – was still prevalent during the early 1970s.

Miss Jane did bother! Her school was fortunate to employ an excellent teacher of French, Mrs Revell-Smith, who was a French national. . . . [Together they] set about devising a syllabus that would guard against such problems and deficiencies for Hampshire pupils. It was agreed that the 45 minute period of the School timetables were of little or no use in helping to attain this vocabulary – the pupils, rushing from one subject to another, often forgot most of what they had learned in the previous class sessions. Obviously, it was desirable to allocate more time and to give greater exposure to the teaching of French – again, more easily stated than achieved. Other examination subjects demanded so much time . . .

The solution to the problem appeared to be to found a 'sister' school somewhere in France. Miss Jane and her husband decided to seek and buy a venue there where all pupils aged eight years and above could spend at least ten days annually and where they could be taught in some depth by qualified French nationals. Miss Jane envisaged a boarding-school programme in which children would work on the French language for three hours each morning, giving special attention to the vocabulary of their environment and the acquisition of correct accents. The singing of songs in French is particularly helpful in the production of [a] good accent. They would assist the *femme de ménage* in household tasks and learn something of cuisine and cooking from a French chef. The afternoons would be spent in visits to places of historic interest, [such as] châteaux, markets [and] farms [to show the local way of life] and leisure facilities in the locality [like swimming and canoeing] – on occasions joining with French children in entertainments and sports. Everything would be geared to assisting the British children to absorb a lasting knowledge of France and its language, customs, culture and people.

[It was] planned for the group visits to France to be made during normal term-time, with the pupils being escorted by their own form teachers. There would be no additional costs to parents for the visits, as these would be seen and accepted as an integral part of school life – the School fee structure in England including all costs for travel, tuition, accommodation and insurance for all of those pupils of eight years and over. Only personal pocket-money would have to be found.

This then was the dream, or plan, on which the scheme would be based – curriculum and objectives to be achieved. What remained was to find a suitable property with an infrastructure which could be the foundation for the plan – as well as the essential administrative work of forming a French company, seeking approval of the French Ministries of Education and Finance and of the many regional and local authorities which form the formidable bureaucracy of school life in France.

Undeterred, [they] began their search for a location for a school, but the immediate difficulty was that Miss Jane could spare so little time from the management of the Schools in London.

It was decided to devote our Easter holidays to search over a period of a few years, but at almost every turn there was frustration. An affordable property with the right amounts of space and services did not seem to exist. From these forays we returned home depressed but never defeated. Much later I wrote of the long search:

> We made up our minds to cull every newspaper advertisement we could find published in England and France. We had considered the Dordogne region but felt that communications and travel would be difficult. However, after reading a very small advertisement in *The Sunday Telegraph* in 1976, we concentrated on that beautiful part of France and decided to respond to the advertisement during the Spring half-term. We knew that the eastern Dordogne was full of history and that there were many places of interest suitable for cultural visits. A school in the Périgord was a possibility!

Keith Wilson was the estate agent who had advertised for sale a group of four pre-revolution buildings in the Périgord Noir in a village called Veyrines-de-Domme. So we contacted him and he sent us this description of the area we were going to see:

> The Périgord Noir is situated in the Départment of the Dordogne south of the Périgord Blanc and to the east of the Périgord Pourpre in the south west of France. It is called 'Noir' because of the countryside covered with oaks and pines which give it a sombre perspective. The leaf cover is dense in the Salardais, the area around Salat, which is crossed by the valleys of the Rivers Dordogne and Vézère. At this point, the valley of the Dordogne is wider than that of the Vézère. Both rivers are fast flowing and in the past have caused massive flooding. But since the construction of the dams in the Haut Dordogne they are fewer now. It was these regular floodings over the centuries which gave the valleys their rich alluvial soil – so good for crop agriculture. It's a very beautiful area sparsely populated in which one would be happy to live.

Keith Wilson's photograph of the area.

It sounded idyllic, so we flew to Bordeaux, the nearest airport about 130 miles from Veyrines, hired a car and wended our way through the lovely vineyards of St Emilion, and along the River Dordogne, following it eastwards to St Cyprien to find a tiny community called Veyrines-de-Domme, just four kilometres south of the River Dordogne.

View along the River Dordogne.

In St Cyprien we met Keith Wilson, the agent who was selling this empty farm *domaine*. We were guided along the winding road (D50), through twisting and hilly country lanes to arrive in the centre of the village, and to see a collection of ruined buildings which stood around the *place* (square). Goodness gracious me! What a sight met our eyes! On seeing the ruins we nearly abandoned the idea altogether!

Photograph of the mas *from the* place, *1977.*

Keith Wilson, however, was used to seeing the neglected buildings in the local area at that time. He persuaded us to stay and take a better look. He told us that the *mas* (farmhouse) predated the revolution and that under the grey *crépissage* (roughcast) was lovely yellow limestone waiting to be revealed. He also mentioned that German troops had occupied the village during the last war – guarding some 180 prisoners, including slave-labourers and deserters from occupied countries. The prisoners lived a dreadful life, working in the local lignite and limestone mines at the nearby village of Allas-les-Mines. They slept in the *domaine* building while the guards were housed in the adjoining building (now the *mairie*), which had been built by the prisoners after normal work. The officers lived in some comfort up on the hill in the tiny sub-hamlet of La Raze. As we stared at the large farmhouse, barn and outbuildings the agent was telling us that the property we were considering purchasing had not been occupied since the end of the war. It was no wonder that the buildings were in such a neglected state. In front of the main building was a large ash tree riven by lightning, and what used to be the village well and wash place.

Whatever our misgivings, we were persuaded to take a better look. After all, we had travelled so far – why not examine the property and site more fully! The agent also encouraged us by saying the whole site was going very cheaply. Persuaded by Keith Wilson to take a better look, we went up a small overgrown *chemin rural*, which ran beside the buildings. As we walked up the lane, we saw in front of us part of a grey-looking building, which turned out to be the former village bakehouse.

Watercolour of the bakehouse,
taken from a 1977 photograph.

To the right of the bakehouse were two stone pillars and a pair of ironwork gates – originally magnificent but now rusting away. They enclosed a *cour* (courtyard) filled with overgrown stinging nettles and even taller brambles! At the far end of the courtyard was a huge ancient *grange* (barn). Its wooden doors and windows were rotting away. However, the building overall made a very strong and promising statement.

My impression of the weed-filled courtyard.

If we had anticipated seeing a beautiful group of Périgordin stone houses, then we were to be bitterly disappointed. By the gates was an ancient *four* (oven) with a leaning bakehouse chimney and the courtyard was full of briars, nettles and weeds – chest- and head-high in some places. In one corner was a ruined *porcherie* (pigsty).

My first impression of the pigsty.

Through the gates one could see the farmhouse, which formed the fourth side of the courtyard. Although severely neglected, the strength of the original architecture again made a definite impression. Although we did not realise it at the time, the farmhouse was originally two buildings. The keystone above the door to the farmhouse bore the date 1782, so they were built just before the revolution.

The farmhouse.

The huge *grange* stretched right across the end of the
courtyard. It was in a poor state although constructed in typical
Périgordin style – roofed with traditional Périgordin tiles
supported below by *lauzes*. These are crafted limestone tiles,

which were still then very common in ancient buildings in 1977. When the roof was restored our *lauzes* miraculously disappeared! This was a pity because they were valuable to the building industry and to us!

Despite their neglected state, the buildings were attractive in their uncompromising honesty, and typical of a Périgordin farm *domaine* of their age. I felt they could be restored to provide a viable and practical venue for a small school – something very different and exciting for our pupils.

We retreated to look at the farmhouse from a different perspective. It had started to snow. The buildings looked on to the village square and we had to decide whether to pursue our interest in this set of buildings or not.

Watercolour titled Looking in 1977 at the Prospect from the Village Square.

Whatever the state of decay, this property in a rural district of the Dordogne offered sanctuary to me, and the knowledge that my pupils would be safe. This was no whimsical or sentimental fancy but a necessary consideration. It must be recalled that

25

in the 1970s the Knightsbridge area had suffered from a number of political and terrorist incidents which had affected the schools. The siege of the Iranian Embassy caused the upper school at Ennismore Gardens to close for four days. A policewoman had been tragically killed by an IRA bomb very close to St Saviour's Hall. From the windows of Ennismore Gardens one was able to see a file of Libyans being deported by a squad of London police officers.

These events underline the fact that, before taking on a school in France, it was imperative to determine the safety and security of children boarding 700 miles from their homes in England. This was my main consideration. The peace and tranquillity was another important factor in the decision of whether to buy or not. There were many other things to be taken into account as well. I thought that the site had potential, although lacking in land area, but we could not ignore the fact that there would be a daunting amount of work (and associated cost) involved in developing these existing building shells into an operating school. While we were pondering these difficulties outside in the village square, we were getting frozen so we all decided to go back to Keith Wilson's office in Berbiguières, to discuss the matter further in the warmth.

When we arrived the first question we asked Wilson was "How much do you think the restoration would cost?"

He replied, "About £200,000."

"How did you arrive at that figure?" we asked.

"Do you realise that the buildings have no electricity, only one water tap and no sewage outlets, for starters?" he explained, and went on to add that the buildings were listed and so planning permission would be needed from the Bureau de Beaux Arts. An architect would have to be employed to make up plans and get the permissions for school use. This architect would have to liaise closely with the Bureau de Beaux Arts and to speak French.

We thought for a moment and asked a second question: "Do

26

you think that the Maire and his *conseils* (councillors) and the commune would welcome an English school in its midst?"

He replied that he would speak to *Monsieur le Maire*.

We thanked him.

He asked us if we realised that all over the region many lovely buildings were falling into decay, and he told us that without an influx of money they were likely to continue to do so. He added that he felt that, in the present climate, they had little hope of being rescued. Of course, at that period the English had not yet discovered the Dordogne and its delights!

We thanked him and said we would give him our decision the following week. Then, leaving behind a somewhat bewildered agent, we set off to enjoy a wonderful Périgordin meal before making our way back to Bordeaux and London.

When we were back in London we gave considerable thought to the village of Veyrines. It contained very few buildings apart from the farm *domaine*. There was a dilapidated *mairie*, a little church, a presbytery, and four farms and their outbuildings. On the hill above the village was the *ecole primaire*. The farmhouses were typical of the local architecture, with their external iron or stone staircases leading up to the first floor, where the families lived. Animals and machinery were to be found on the ground floor, and the lofts above the living quarters were used for hay and other storage. The gardens were small and appeared well tended. Every farmer had land round the village, and kept a few animals. We had been informed that most of the villagers had been born there, and their families had lived there for centuries. At that time, in 1977, no house had indoor facilities. It was nearly ten years later when bathrooms were installed inside.

We decided to do some research about the Dordogne region before confirming the purchase. It appeared that the hamlet of Veyrines was well hidden in *La France Profonde* at that

27

time. The River Dordogne is one of the five great rivers of France; it is one of the longest, being about 500 kilometres long, flowing west to reach the Atlantic Ocean, via the Garonne and the Gironde. The source of the River Dordogne is in the Massif Central at the jagged peak Puy de Sancy. Balzac described this peak brilliantly in his novel *La Peau de Chagrin*.

The valley of the River Dordogne.

One of the books we were recommended to read in researching the area was *The Generous Earth*, written in 1950, in which Philip Oyler described an area still unknown to many people at that time. We particularly liked the following passage:

At my feet the limestone which underlies this whole region, ended with a perpendicular cliff at 1000 feet and I looked over the Dordogne valley, a mile or more across, to seemingly endless hills beyond, with its wide clear river, still in places, and with mirrored spires of poplars in it, forming islands and small cascades. In the valley I could see countless little homesteads, innumerable plots of cultivation. Near the river itself and on the slopes adjoining were lush looking pastures. Up the

*Watercolour of the Puy de Sancy in the Massif Central,
where the River Dordogne rises.*

steeper slopes were vineyards above them the woods, which reached up to the top of the hills, wherever the sides were not too steep for a tree to find footing. It was a panorama which spelt wealth to me, true wealth. All was bounty and beauty. God-given and man had not desecrated it.

From our guidebooks we learnt that although Veyrines was still fairly isolated, it was close to many wonderful and attractive sites. This, for our educational purpose, was a definite plus. There were the wonderful medieval towns of Sarlat and St Cyprien; the famous châteaux of Beynac on the north side of the river and Castelnaud facing it on the south side; Domme, a French fortified town known as a bastide; and many limestone caves, all within easy driving distance of the proposed school.

We reconsidered the fact that almost no one had heard of Veyrines-de-Domme at that time – that is, apart from the 200 inhabitants of the commune whose families had lived and farmed there for centuries. It really was a hamlet in La France Profonde! For us it was the beautiful surrounding countryside with its unspoilt rurality that persuaded us to purchase. We knew that total immersion in a rural French way of life would provide our pupils from London with a wonderful and different educational experience. It would be a great opportunity for our pupils to learn in a non-touristic way about another country, and to speak its language.

From London we rang Keith Wilson to ask if he had spoken to Maire Frances and to discover the response. The Maire was agreeable and even delighted at the thought that his commune would benefit from an injection of cash and more people in his community. So we told Keith Wilson we wanted to purchase the site and asked him to arrange for the appropriate papers, etc.

At last our search was over! There was, however, a great deal of hard work to follow before the buildings could house pupils and staff and become a school.

Chapter 4

The Hard Work Begins

David Lemmon writes:

The purchase of the site at Veyrines-de-Domme was completed in 1977, with L'Ecole Hampshire, SARL (Société à Responsabilité Limitée) being registered as a limited company and subsidiary of Hampshire Tutorials Limited, the service company operating Ennismore Gardens and St Saviour's Hall. But it was not all 'plain sailing' in any respect. A vast amount of legal and administrative work was still to be done. Lawyers, notaries, accountants and consultants based in Paris, Bordeaux and Sarlat strove (at astonishingly high fees) to pilot the enterprise through the treacherous waters of French administrations. Eventually the Ministries of Education and Finance, the authorities for employment and social security, the Département de la Dordogne, Pensions Boards, the Direction Générale des Impôts, the local Registre du Commerce, and seemingly endless other bodies *all* approved L'Ecole Hampshire and its directors as being legitimate. But this was achieved only after sundry officials and legal representatives had sworn affidavits that Madame Jane Box-Grainger was a fit and proper person to care for children and conduct the enterprise under the moral laws of France! . . .

L'Ecole Hampshire, with Miss Jane as Gérante, became recognised as legal and acceptable. But even then, the Mayor of the little commune . . . had to countersign various documents giving his overriding approval.

The next step was to engage an architect, and we found Johnny Devas. He was a cousin of some three pupils who had attended the London School in the middle of the 1950s. His nationality was Anglo-French, and he lived in the Lot–Quercy region about two hours' drive from the school. He was expert in ancient-building restoration work, and could liaise quite happily with the Bureau de Beaux Arts in Périgueux, whose officials proved to be invaluable in helping to restore the buildings to very nearly their original appearance, and in advising on costs and materials. I don't think we could have succeeded without Johnny Devas' knowledge, skills and local contacts. When he put his very imaginative and thorough plans to the authority they were finally passed, after a visit to France.

One day we received an urgent phone call from our architect, Johnny Devas: "Come to France at once!"

On receiving the telephone call, I panicked. Were we about to lose the property? I knew the timely payment for the planning permissions was vital if we were going to be able to continue with this project, so I dropped everything, booked a flight and flew to Toulouse, near to Johnny's home, on the Friday evening. Very early on the Saturday morning Johnny Devas came to meet us at our hotel in Toulouse. He showed me what and where we had to sign, and we paid any outstanding dues. Disaster was averted and we received permission to use the farm *domaine* as a school. I dread to imagine what would have happened if Johnny had not been so alert and conscientious. There would have been no sister school in France.

Having done so much work, and with considerable expense, we now had to get the local *notaire* to confirm the purchase. Sadly we had to wait nearly a whole year because the first *notaire* had to resign hurriedly due to ill health, and the second was killed in a car accident. But when the year was nearly up we managed to get an appointment with a *notaire* in Belvès who was ready to seal the contract.

Belvès is a very ancient town occupying a promontory over the River Nauze about twenty minutes from Veyrines. The *notaire*'s office was tiny, but Christopher Huet (our legal representative), my husband and I, Keith Wilson and the Maire of Veyrines all managed to squeeze in – just! The documents were signed; the francs were passed to the *notaire*, including the appropriate taxes. In France the buyer pays the taxes and the *notaire* keeps the deeds of the property until the buildings are sold on again. When all was signed and sealed, we retired to a local *hostellerie* to refresh ourselves in the traditional manner.

Chapter 5

Restoration

Now at last we owned the *domaine*, and with all the planning consents in place we could start the restoration works. This was really urgent because there is usually heavy rain in late autumn in the Dordogne region, and this would do even more damage to the neglected buildings. Therefore it was imperative to get the work started as soon as possible, to protect the buildings and our investment.

The first stage of the restoration was to clear the courtyard of weeds, brambles and debris. The debris seen in the photo opposite has come in part from the destruction of the bakehouse and pigsty, which were cleared to make a new house for the principal so I could stay in situ on my visits. There had been a lot of rain during the winters of 1978 and 1979, and on one visit we were devastated to see the damage done to the *grange*, and the foundations of my house were at least 18 inches deep in water!

The work progressed well. How promising the *grange* looked with its new roof and *pierres jaunes* revealed! And how fortunate we were to have such excellent workmen and stonemasons!

Photograph showing the debris in the courtyard as it was being cleared and the storm damage to the grange *roof.*

The courtyard had been excavated to hold all the service pipes. Putting these service pipes (water, electricity, sewage and telephone) underground allowed the beauty of the architecture to be seen fully, which justified the extra expense.

Distressingly, the ground floor filled with water during the winter rains because the roofers were tardy. This did not happen again with the other buildings, because the contractors were asked to agree to a strict timetable before getting the contract. Even though we put under-floor heating in the house, there is still damp penetration on the lane side today!

During 1979 we found problems which had to be tackled and solved. We realised when we purchased the ruined farm *domaine* that there would be considerable difficulties which would have to be faced and overcome.

Watercolour showing restoration of the grange *in progress.*

The bakehouse and pigsty being transformed into the principal's house at an early stage.

Watercolour showing how the little house looked from the chemin rural.

First, the tiny village had a small pipe to feed its few houses with water, but the proposed influx of people for a school would require a greater volume of water. The Maire was very helpful. He organised with SOGEDA SA for a new, larger, pipe to be installed for the village. It proved to be a most satisfactory solution then, and it still supplies the school more than thirty years later!

Secondly, the village had only single-phase electricity. One has to remember Veyrines had no street lighting in 1979. Single-phase electricity could never have supplied the school with power, not only for heating and light, but also for the use of a language laboratory. The solution was to arrange with EDF for the school to have its own *poste*, which would provide sufficient electricity for its own needs. Pylons were erected over the hills to carry on overhead wires the electricity to our newly erected *poste,* situated behind the principal's house then in the process of being constructed. Seven thousand pounds was the cost in 1979; I wonder how much it would cost today? The village today has street lighting for its sole street, and some villagers' houses have modern electrical equipment – although some villagers have preferred to resist the change and the cost!

Veyrines had no sewage system. All the few dwellings used cesspits. Obviously for a school housing forty-plus people this was an impractical solution. In World War II the *domaine* had housed up to 180 prisoners of war – but how those poor devils managed I don't know! The village was remote and in rural France after all! When the Maire and his *conseils* had been consulted by Johnny Devas, a *convention* was arranged and signed to permit the new school to use a small piece of commune land outside the *grange* in the village square. On this land was to be installed a Pompe Oxyfor – a pump to purify the sewage from the school. It had twelve stations, and the school agreed to give the Maire use of three of them for his offices and the *salle des fêtes*. The pump was to be paid for by the school and Oxyfor SA from Toulose would fit it. The purified water would travel through excavation pipes to be placed under the village square. The clean water would enter an existing stream below the village. The cost of this work, which included making good the village square, would be for paid by the Maire.

In 1978 there was only a single telephone link with the village, and this was connected to the Maire's office. A telephone is an essential means of communication for a school, so it was arranged for us to have a link from the Maire's line to a *poste* on the edge of the school *domaine*. France Télécom SA was engaged to supply the line and the *poste* which linked the school to the village system. Much later a public telephone box was installed below the *mairie* in the village square.

A serious problem arose with the supervision of the restoration works. The supervisor is called a *maître d'oeuvres*. He organises and supervises all the different tradesmen working on the project. In France, each tradesman is qualified only to work in his own special trade. Thus a *maître d'oeuvres*, is very necessary to the progress of a building project. The problem was that Johnny Devas, who had combined the work of architect and *maître d'oeuvres*, found that travelling to and from his home two hours away was very time-consuming and, for us, very costly. So sadly we released Johnny and looked for a replacement.

We were offered Claude Teulet – a relation of the Holt Family, who had two children in the London School. Claude lived only ten minutes away from Veyrines and was free to start work at once. We accepted the offer gratefully and he became our new *maître d'oeuvres*. The first problem which he had to solve was termite infestation in most of the wood, including the *poutres* (roof beams). He advised us to take out a twenty-year contract against further damage. However, the damage was already so far advanced in much of the wood that it had to be destroyed. All the *poutres* in the left-hand side of the farmhouse, facing the village square, had to be replaced. All the new wood was treated under this contract. Meanwhile restoration work continued on the farmhouse.

Watercolour of the work getting under way.

Watercolour of the side of the farmhouse
facing the village square.

In the previous picture one can see a certain amount of excavated debris in front of the building. The original doors and windows were still visible at this stage. On the top floor one can see the entrance for the pigeons to the loft. In the completed building this entrance was blocked from behind, and the loft was converted into a dormitory, with its own showers and lavatory.

Watercolour of the grange *before restoration, showing its entrance into the village square.*

Prior to our purchase, the villagers had, for many years, used the *grange* to dry tobacco before sending it to SEITA in

Bergerac for processing. The walnut crop, which was harvested later, was dried in the *grange* and shelled. The shell husks were sent to be used by the aerospace industry. The entrance from the *grange* into the village square was closed in the restoration.

During the restoration of the farmhouse something most unusual was discovered. We had to excavate to make rooms with enough ceiling height for dining rooms and kitchens, so we had to dig down into the foundations and remove soil and debris. In the course of this work three skeletons were discovered, so the work was brought to a halt and the authorities were called in to analyse the skeletons. After some weeks, it was decided that these remains came from the Middle Ages – perhaps they were buried away from the church as they were heretics. The remains were removed to the cemetery, after permission was granted by the authorities.

The following is my translation of an article which appeared in the *Sud Ouest*:

Working on the excavations to lower the ground level, two brothers, Jean and Liviani Mounet, were using their pickaxes when, suddenly, the tip of one of the pickaxes struck something which turned out to be the remains of a skull. They told the other labourers, who were working on the house situated close to the church in Veyrines-de-Domme. Carefully they released the skeleton from the ground – definitely a woman with her arms folded across her shoulders. They continued to dig around the hole and found two other skeletons – obviously a man from his physique and another older man.

It is almost certain that the skeletons came from the Middle Ages because of their burial in the house. Perhaps they were the bodies of heretics or people who had been tortured and who did not have the right to be buried in holy ground.

Some specialists came to discover the causes of their death. A doctor also came to organise their removal and to determine how they died – seven or eight centuries ago.

A Veyrines-de-Domme
Trois squelettes
venus du Moyen Age

Des travaux dans le sous-sol d'une maison. Jean et Liviani Mounet — ils sont frères — piochent le sol lorsque, soudain, leur pelle bute sur ce qu'ils croient être une toupine. En fait il s'agit d'un crâne humain.

A deux pas de l'église

Ils font part de leur découverte à leurs camarades de chantier, qui travaillent avec eux dans cette maison située à deux pas de l'église de Veyrines-de-Domme. Et avec précaution, ils dégagent un squelette, sans doute celui d'une femme, les bras repliés sur les épaules.

Ils continuent à creuser alentour et dégagent deux autres squelettes dont l'un correspond visiblement au physique d'un homme dans la force de l'âge.

Il est à peu près probable qu'il faille chercher au Moyen Age au plus tôt la raison de la présence d'une sépulture dans cette maison. Peut-être sont-ce les corps des suppliciés ou d'hérétiques, en tout cas de personnes qui n'étaient pas admises à reposer en terre bénie dans le cimetière.

Les causes de la mort

Or, celui-ci est tout proche. Des spécialistes diront ce qu'il faut penser de cette découverte. C'est ainsi que la venue d'un médecin — qui se déplacera à titre personnel — est attendue avec impatience pour tenter de déterminer les causes de la mort de ces trois personnes... il y a sept ou huit siècles.

Un des squelettes.

(Ph. Lucien Roulland)

Photograph and report from the Sud Ouest.

The restoration work was restarted immediately; however, another problem arose. We heard unsatisfactory reports about the new *maître d'oeuvres*, and finally Claude had a blazing row with one of the contractors, and he had to be persuaded to leave our employment.

We were extremely fortunate to find Bernard Devaux, an architect who lived about twenty minutes away at Marnac.

43

He came to our rescue and finished the project. He was a wise and tactful man, and he managed the project very well.

Photograph from the Sud Ouest *of the workmen who discovered the skeletons.*

It appeared that our budget of £200,000 for the restoration works was woefully inadequate. In fact, a further £200,000 was required to complete the project.

Why was our budget incorrect? Here are some of the reasons:

1. The agent, Keith Wilson, gave us an estimate of costs which was too low, either because he was not an expert in restoration costs, or because he didn't want to deter us from purchasing the *domaine*.

2. While we had restored fifteenth-century cottages in Sandwich, Kent, and made improvements to 63 Ennismore Gardens, we were inexperienced in restoration projects this size – especially in the heart of the Dordogne, 700 miles from London.

3. We had to rely on an architect and two *maître d'oeuvre*s to oversee the project far from home. This proved to be expensive, but we had to employ people to supervise the project when our own work at home made it impossible for us to be in France full-time.

4. We had to accept estimates for work which were possibly too high, in an effort to complete the project.

5. Our regular visits to the site, involving air travel, hotels and car hire, were at times costly, especially as we could travel only when our work schedule in England allowed.

When we saw that we were about to overrun the original budget we looked at other properties near Veyrines. In almost every case the properties had been left unfinished due to lack of funds! We realised that a half-finished project – no matter how much hard work had already been done – was in fact, at that time, unsaleable. Therefore we decided to take on a loan and complete our buildings so that if we had to sell, there would be something to sell.

We decided to keep these problems to ourselves because we did not want to worry the parents and staff in our London schools. Fortunately our accountant, Ron Rawstron, FCA, recommended Stephen Mitchell to approach Barclays Bank on my behalf for a loan. After all, the school had no mortgage or borrowing and I owned a valuable freehold in Knightsbridge, so why not ask the bank to lend me the money? A meeting was arranged and a loan of £180,000 was agreed against the deeds of Ennismore Gardens. In return the bank expected income and expenditure accounts to be sent to them each month until the loan was repaid.

The loan was used for the following:

1. Removal of the *crépissage* (the roughcast covering the original stones). This had to be chipped off by hand – a laborious and lengthy task.

2. Repairs to the boundary wall between the Lalbat building and the school garden to prevent rain coming down the hill behind and flooding the kitchen.

3. A small secondary wall to protect the farmhouse. This was built, leaving a passage between the farmhouse and the garden, with some grids for the rainwater to escape. By this means the problem was solved and the ground floor of the farmhouse remained unflooded.

4. New ironwork entrance gates.

5. Wooden shutters for all the twenty-five windows and the doors on to the village square.

6. A grid and shale wall to protect the Pompe Oxyfor.

7. Building and planting the garden inside the courtyard and the garden furniture.

8. Making a patio for the principal's house.

9. Employing a locksmith to make all the doors to the building secure.

10. Building a tennis court.

11. Purchasing two cars and, eventually, two minibuses.

All the external work had to be ratified by the Bureau de Beaux Arts in Périgueux. This added to the costs in some cases but greatly enhanced the finished appearance of the buildings. Then we had to furnish the interiors, which were still empty shells. Before the school could be opened we needed to pay for the following:

1. Linoleum for the ground floor and carpets everywhere else.

2. Ten wash basins, ten lavatories, and six shower rooms with shower curtains, towel rails and mirrors.

3. Beds – fifty in all, with their mattresses and blankets. (The Parents' Association was helpful in making the bedcovers and donating them.)

4. Bedside lockers.

5. Tables – twenty-four in all.

6. Chairs – sixty in all.

7. Laminated workbenches for the three sides of both classrooms.

8. Library shelving in the classrooms and office.

9. Storage cupboards in the classrooms and office.

10. Building a kitchen and providing all the equipment.

11. Audio-visual equipment including televisions.

12. China and cutlery for fifty people and tablecloths.

13. Curtains for most windows.

14. Sports equipment.

15. Games for playing indoors.

16. Library books and textbooks.

17. Pictures to decorate walls to give the place a lived-in appearance.

18. Whiteboards or blackboards.

19. A three-piece suite for the *salon* (sitting room).

20. Refurbishment of the fireplaces in the farmhouse and the principal's office. (It must be noted that nearly all the furniture in the principal's house was imported from England.)

21. Under-floor heating in the principal's house. (Sadly there is still damp penetration on the lane side today.)

The total cost of exterior works and furnishing the interiors was just under half a million pounds.

The Lalbat building was typical of Périgordin architecture – (a building in golden limestone covered by steep sloping roofs of brown tiles and *lauzes)*. Despite the charm of these buildings it was 1990 or even later when toilet facilities were installed indoors.

Watercolour showing the wall now completely repaired. The lovely tiles and the beautiful pigeonnier *of the Lalbat building is visible.*

Chapter 6

The Maires of Veyrines

I should like to thank the Maires of Veyrines for their help and assistance. Here are the names of the maires since our arrival:

Michel Frances (1971–83)
Jean Louis Boisserie (1984–2001)
Yves Delpech (2001–4)
Francis Vierge (2004–present)

All these gentlemen were or are consistently helpful to the school and I am very grateful to them.

In 1977 the *mairie* was on the first floor, reached by an iron staircase. On the ground floor there were some garages or stores with their rusty metal covers. Later these garages became the *salle des fêtes*.

The Maire now has a modern office in the old presbytery on the other side of the village square.

The Maire granted the school some commune land to build a tennis court. This land was situated behind the presbytery on the other side of the village square. The Maire made a

The mairie *in 1977.*

The mairie *in 2007.*

convention to enable the school to use this piece of commune land on five days a week; on the other days it was reserved for use by the commune if they wished. It added greatly to the school's facilities and to our pupils' enjoyment.

The tennis court.

I should also like to say again how helpful we found the Bureau de Beaux Arts in Périgueux. Their advice helped us to develop Grade II listed buildings so that they retained their typical Périgordin style, while at the same time making them viable as a small language school in the heart of France.

I'm happy to report that the village also benefited from the influx of money and provision of work to the local entrepreneurs. A visitor today would hardly recognise the Veyrines of 1977 – a remote village in La France Profonde, untouched at that time by modern life. Today it is a thriving, bustling place while still retaining its old-world charm and rural peace.

Chapter 7

Some Results of the Restoration Works

I think it's time to show how lovely the school looked in 1980 – no longer a ruined farm *domaine,* as it was in 1977!

The fully restored farmhouse seen from the village square.

One of the dormitories.

One of the dining rooms.

Watercolour of the principal's house, built from the old bakehouse and pigsty. What an exciting and charming revelation!

Upstairs there are two bedrooms, a bathroom and a separate lavatory. A new oak staircase was constructed to link the two floors. On the ground floor there is a dining room, a sitting room and a small kitchen.

The sitting room in the principal's house.

The dining room in the principal's house.

Patio leading out to the garden from the sitting room.

Chapter 8

Staffing

The next stage was to find our complement of staff.

The building works had created a lot of local interest in the school; there was a lot of curiosity! That area of the Dordogne has little employment to offer on the whole, so many bilingual people called at the school to find work: teachers, secretaries, chefs, kitchen workers and drivers. As a result, it was not difficult to recruit staff. I intended to run the school and be in France when we had pupils. I knew from my experience of more than fifteen years of running The Hampshire School in London that a few well-chosen staff members was infinitely preferable to a situation where we were overstaffed.

I had to take into account as well that the French system of staff employment and the type of their contracts were rather different from our own. There were two contracts for staff. The first was a *contrat de durée limitée*, which gave starting and ending dates. This was the one I used. The second was a *contrat de durée illimitée*, which gave in broad terms, employment for life! Salaries were documented by *bulletins de paie*, which showed (a) dates and hours worked; (b) holidays; (c) overtime, if any; and (d) deductions for tax and social-security contributions. These documents were sent to my accountant, who then worked out the contributions quarterly. In France there are three separate categories for contributions: first, contributions for unemployment benefit; second, contributions for health; and, finally, contributions for pensions.

After conducting a number of interviews I decided to employ two teachers. Janine Graves was a French national who had previously been married to an Englishman and had lived in England for a number of years. She was qualified and had already taught in English schools for at least seven years. Janine was one of the most fluently bilingual people I interviewed. She also had an extensive knowledge of the local area, which was to prove invaluable when preparing pupils for their afternoon visits. She was offered a seasonal contract – that is, a *contrat de durée limitée*. Her hours of work were 9 a.m. to 12.30 p.m. Mondays to Saturdays inclusive. It also helped that Janine now lived at Le Coux Bigaroux, about 12 kilometres from Veyrines. She was a great asset and worked for the school for more than fifteen years, when she had to retire due to ill health. My second choice was Odette Jardin, a Frenchwoman with many years' experience in teaching in *ecoles primaires*. She lived locally at Castelnaud-la-Chapelle, not far from the school. She was a fully qualified teacher in the French system with an excellent local knowledge. She was offered the same type of contract as Janine, and she accepted. She turned out to be a happy choice.

Communication is a very important part of the school business, and we were lucky to find a secretary in Pippa Ackhurst, who had emigrated to France. She was bilingual and proved to be hard-working, tactful and continuously helpful and understanding. She too accepted a seasonal *contrat de durée limitée*, and her hours of work were from 9 a.m. to 5 p.m. on all the weekdays.

A school providing boarding facilities needs to fill two more important posts: a chef and a *femme de ménage*. Angela

Lalflaquière was my first choice. She was cordon-bleu trained and married to a Frenchman who lived about 20 kilometres away from Veyrines in Siorac-en-Périgord. Angela accepted the contract and was a happy choice at the opening of our new school. She was quickly followed by Georges Pestourie, who had worked as a chef on ships, and in hotels and restaurants and proved to be an adaptable and loyal employee, as well as a wonderful cook. He also accepted a seasonal contract, and his hours of work were 7 a.m. to 4 p.m. Mondays to Sundays inclusive. He provided the French-style p*etit déjeuner*, followed by an excellent three-course lunch. During the morning he prepared supper for the *femme de ménage* to serve at night. Georges lived about 12 kilometres from the school and worked for many years with us.

We were lucky to find Colette Mazet, who had lived in Veyrines all her life. Colette also accepted the seasonal contract. Her hours of work were 8 a.m. to 12 p.m. Mondays to Sundays, and on the weekday evenings from 7 p.m. to 10 p.m. Her morning work included helping the chef in the kitchen as well as cleaning the school. Her evening work was preparing the supper provided by the chef and washing up afterwards.

On Sunday evenings we used to take pupils either to local restaurants or on picnics. The picnics on the whole proved much more popular.

Another find was Diana Leseigneur, a multilingual Frenchwoman. She was a great asset in translating my questionnaires on the cultural visits from English into French.

Her husband, Bernard, was an excellent driver whom we employed. We needed drivers for the afternoon visits, and they were paid hourly when required. Pippa also helped with driving, as I did myself on occasions.

Supervision of groups in the dormitories, and during the afternoons and evenings, was performed by escorting teachers or group leaders. They had every morning free with the free use of the school cars, but on Sundays the escorting teachers or group leaders were on supervision duty all day. They were paid by their own organisation or school.

For the holiday groups I employed two monitors for four-week periods at a time. They were normally paid in pounds sterling as they came from England, but they were invariably fluent in French.

English was usually taught by myself. However, when we had a lot of students in the holidays studying English, I employed a second teacher – an Englishman who was living in France.

Apart from managing the school and being on site all the time when we had pupils, I did any odd jobs required. I took no salary in France during the whole period from 1977 to 1993. This management style, although hard on me at times, maintained a smooth and successful project.

Three staff members: Janine, Odette and me.

It was necessary to show my new staff the basic timetable and syllabus which I had prepared. It was also necessary to show the parents and staff of The Hampshire School this extension to their pupils' syllabus. Thus we prepared a prospectus, which showed not only the new school's facilities but some photographs of the local area. The prospectus was bilingual, French and English (see Appendix IV).

In 1981, although The Hampshire School groups arrived on a regular basis, they could not fill the school throughout the year. It was necessary to encourage other schools to join us in term time. During the holidays we had individual pupils between the ages of eight and seventeen from many places worldwide. The new prospectus was very helpful to our recruitment of groups and individual pupils.

Photograph taken from the prospectus, showing a group of young pupils studying in the grange, *now converted into a large and spacious classroom.*

When the school was not being used by other groups, small adult groups were used to fill the dates; but as more school groups took up dates we had no more rooms for the adults, sadly. We started adult courses with French in the morning, and special cookery lessons with Georges as part of their afternoon programme. The adult groups much enjoyed the cultural visits and local restaurants, whether they used their own transport or were ferried to the venues by the school.

Adult groups studying in the school.

Chapter 9

Syllabus and Timetable

Before coming to Veyrines, I had given a lot of thought to how to provide an exciting educational experience for pupils and staff here in France and to create a syllabus and timetable specifically tailored to the region and teaching French and English as foreign languages. I decided to use a *laboratoire de langues* (language laboratory). With television's special teaching programmes, it was an invaluable aid, though at that time it was considered forward-thinking and modern. The timetable we devised played a very important role in making the curriculum easily absorbed at all levels, without too many hiccups!

It was very important that the courses studied by our pupils committed them to achieve as much 'total immersion' as possible during their course.

Timetable of Morning Study

9 a.m.–11 a.m.   Lessons, including vocabulary work, reading, listening and attempting conversation. With or without use of the language laboratory, morning

work included a brief outline of the cultural visits planned for the afternoon as part of their curriculum. In both classrooms there was a map of the area, because preparation for the cultural visit in the afternoon session was essential as a link between the classroom and the French or English experience. Questionnaires were also in use.

11 a.m.–11.15 a.m. Break period. A tuck shop was available.

11.15 a.m.–12.15 p.m. Television programmes. The younger children benefited from continuous narratives while the more mature students preferred actual programmes from French television, which we videoed in advance. All programmes included questionnaires.

"Three hours of French or English!" you cry. "Weren't the pupils exhausted or bored?"

On occasion, of course, yes – but, on the whole, certainly not! The pupils were young on average and so were fresher in the morning and more ready to absorb lessons. They found it easier to remember when they were immersed for continuous periods in a programme of the language they were studying. These hours proved not only to be successful but very productive.

Drawing by a young pupil of her class enjoying the final morning's session. The teaching video Muzzy was much enjoyed by the young and was an effective teaching method at the end of the morning.

The afternoons would involve getting out and about, which was paramount not only in extending the pupils' knowledge of the language, but also for getting a real feel for France and its culture. This also introduced a holiday mood into the curriculum because all successful learning experiences involve capturing the pupils' interest and therefore their enjoyment! The students used to look forward to the afternoon work as a different and refreshing way to study, or simply for having fun, so only some of the visits were cultural, while others included sporting activities and shopping.

The Périgord Noir is full of exciting possibilities for visits. However, it was important for the choices to be reasonably local to Veyrines because the enthusiasm of the young can evaporate quite quickly. Long journeys by coach or minibus could, as one pupil so succinctly put it, 'bore us rigid'!

The return home was followed by 'homework' for thirty minutes. Sometimes it included questionnaires which the school had made either in English or French. At other times, the pupils illustrated their visits. Some examples of their work are included in Appendix I.

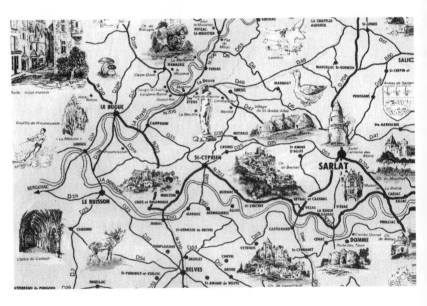

A pictorial view of the area around Veyrines. Maps like this one were displayed in the classrooms.

Chapter 10

Leisure Activities During the Afternoons

The following pages show some of our leisure activities, which contributed greatly to the education and enjoyment of pupils. These activities gave them a good view of the local area and a chance to practise their language skills.

HORSE RIDING

Riding was a wonderful way to enjoy the unspoilt countryside.

Some illustrations by some young 'horsy' pupils.

COOKING

Georges' English was not very good but he was an excellent chef and good with the young. The pupils enjoyed the lessons and it was a very good exercise in understanding the language and proving it by demonstrating their cooking skills.

Pour 6 personnes :
Préparation : 10 min
Cuisson : 45 min
Ingrédients :
100 g de farine
125 g de beurre
4 œufs
300 g de sucre
250 g de cerneaux de noix
1 cuillerée à soupe de rhum
Sucre glace

Préparation :
Préchauffer le four Th 6 (180°).
Mélanger le beurre fondu, la farine tamisée, le sucre et les jaunes d'oeuf. Piler les cerneaux de noix et les ajouter à la préparation.

Battre les blancs en neige très ferme et les incorporer au mélange, puis ajouter le rhum. Verser dans un moule à manqué et enfourner pour 45 minutes environ.

Démouler sur un plat de service, saupoudrer de sucre glace. Se sert tiède ou à température ambiante, mais surtout pas à la sortie du réfrigérateur !

Délicieux avec une Crème anglaise... ou des fraises fraîches...

SWIMMING

We swam at Parc des Milandes or in the River Dordogne from July to September. During the hot and warm weather the pupils often preferred to swim instead of visiting local sites, so we allowed them to choose. When we had English and French pupils at the same time, the activity was particularly effective in their language development as well!

At Parc des Milandes.

CANOEING

Mr Roqueoff provided the canoes, lifejackets and instructors for our groups. His team was wonderful and all the pupils had huge enjoyment, even if they were nervous at first – in fact, so much so that if they had the opportunity to canoe twice in a visit, you could hear the resounding cries of "Yippee! Yippee!"

Photograph featured in the Sud Ouest *newspaper.*

Our pupils canoeing down the Dordogne passed a most spectacular village – La Roque Gageac. Many of the houses cling to an impressive cliff overlooking the river. The cliff provides a microclimate, and tropical palms and cacti flourish between the little houses.

Watercolour of La Roque Gageac.

Canoeing on the Dordogne.

Picture of canoeing, by Neville Maher (aged 9).

Odette Jardin and I conducting games in the village square – French and English children learning and mixing together.

Pupils from the ecole primaire *with a group from The Hampshire School, playing musical chairs in one of the classrooms after tea.*

Happy holiday groups of both English and French pupils. The English studied French in the mornings, while the French studied English. During the afternoons, they did activities together and communicated with each other. Their ages ranged from ten to seventeen.

Chapter 11

Progress Report

The preceding chapters have shown that L'Ecole Hampshire was up and running, ready to accept pupils from its parent school in Knightsbridge and other schools, by the spring of 1981.

We pressed on to open the school fully in May 1982. It was the culmination of nearly four years of very hard and expensive work, but I have never regretted a minute of it, nor a penny of it. In that time we spent nearly every weekend in buying and fitting kitchens, toilets or electrical equipment and making all the other dozens of arrangements necessary to establish a language and boarding school for some forty pupils and staff.

Organised with much care, the courses are designed to teach the English to communicate easily with the people of France in their streets, shops, schools and homes. Similarly, the French were taught to communicate in everyday English.

Pupils came from Cameron House School, Garden House School, Falkner House and Lady Eden's School in London; Bedales Schools in Hampshire; Northfield School in Hertfordshire; Hall Grove School and Reigate St Mary's School in Surrey; Broadwater Manor School in West Sussex;

and Downe House School in Berkshire. Pupils also came from Ireland, France, Spain, Portugal, Italy, Belgium and Germany – and as far afield as Kenya, Madagascar, Mexico, Trinidad, Canada and the USA. At L'Ecole Hampshire the pupils all live and play together in harmony and safety – learning during the mornings and then enjoying swimming, riding, canoeing and cultural visits during the afternoons.

After ten years (and an investment of some £500,000) L'Ecole Hampshire was fully established and successful. Since the first course in July 1980, some 4,000 students had attended the school, enjoying the courses, the sports and the extramural activities provided on an inclusive basis. L'Ecole Hampshire had featured widely in newspapers, including *The Times*, the *Times Educational Supplement*, the *Daily Telegraph*, *The Independent*, the *Wall Street Journal* and *The American* in Britain and the USA; and *Le Monde*, the *Sud Ouest*, *Vocable* and *L'Essor Sarladaise* in France. The school had also featured on Radio Périgord, and had become a recognised force in Anglo-French educational circles. Expolangues in Paris was attended to promote the school two years running.

The dream had been realised. The whole educational project had been exciting and very worthwhile, and I have always been glad that we settled in Veyrines-de-Domme in the heart of the Dordogne.

But what of the school's future?

Pippa and I at Expolangues in Paris.

Chapter 12

A Change Occurs

The Hampshire School made their bookings very late in 1991. Our bookings for school groups were increasing all the time, and the dates The Hampshire School wanted were not available, so I offered to put them in the Centre de Jeunesse, about fifteen minutes from the school, and to provide all the teaching and accommodation as before. However, the headmaster thought that the 'youth hostel' was inferior – in fact, the venue and facilities were as good as my own. I had retired from The Hampshire School in 1986–7, and the reason why the bookings had increased in France was because I had more time to devote to the French school. So my old school decided to look for another venue for their 'French Experience'. It was a great sadness to me that things had not worked out to our mutual satisfaction.

Meanwhile, Sue Cameron came to see L'Ecole Hampshire, recommended by Adrian Richardson of Cothill House school. Sue was then head of Downe House School – a famous girls' public school in Berkshire. She arrived as we were preparing the school for our Easter course – without warning! She said that she had been searching far and wide to find a new venue. She told me that she had sent her twelve-year-old girls to Mayenne the year before and she wanted to look at my school with the idea of moving her girls to Veyrines next year. She looked at my beautifully restored buildings, which did not look like the average school. I took her across the courtyard, and when she entered the *grange* and saw the classroom she said, "Oh, it's a proper school!" I then showed her all the dormitories and their facilities, the kitchen, the dining rooms, the second classroom, the office and the *salon*. She seemed pleased and was especially delighted when she saw the tennis court on the other side of the village square. She said she was happy to find a school so well equipped and ready to move into at once.

It was arranged that I should go to Downe House School to meet the governors, to discuss with them the use of my school. The governors decided to rent the school for a year, using my staff, as well as their own houseparents. I accepted their offer because my husband had retired and wanted me to be with him. It therefore suited me to be able to spend more time with him.

Downe House girls in Domme.

79

As I already had bookings for the coming year it was agreed that Downe House School and L'Ecole Hampshire would have shared use of the buildings. Each school would use different weeks or months.

This could have worked, but in practice it didn't. Therefore in 1994 L'Ecole Hampshire agreed to give Downe House School exclusive use of the buildings; L'Ecole Hampshire was to be responsible for the building maintenance only. This arrangement continued until 1997, when an agreement was reached that the property would be purchased. This finally took place in 2005.

Chapter 13

The Downe House Era

In September 1991, the first group of second-year pupils from Downe House School spent a term at a château in France. Many of their lessons were conducted in French, and they were taught by local French teachers whilst being under the care of Downe House School's houseparents.

They enjoyed French sports, visits to nearby places of interest and local events; and they were given the chance to become involved in the life of the community through their project work. It was a highly successful 'experiment', and it has now become a feature of the second year for all girls at Downe House School. Gains in fluency and confidence in French are matched by broader gains in increased self-confidence, the ability to work in a group, and general self-reliance. The base for Downe House School in France is now in the Dordogne, at Veyrines-de-Domme.

I asked Sue Cameron to write something which I could include in this chronicle. She gladly consented, and here is a resumé of what she wrote:

> An idea was germinating. Times had changed, and numbers in the school had increased, so tighter discipline and more formal structure were necessary for success and happy coexistence.

Nevertheless, the qualities extolled by Olive Willis [the founder of Downe House School] were still 'in the woodwork', recognised by Old Seniors as the spirit of the school; indeed they seemed more and more desirable as the twentieth century drew to a close. The concept of a more closely knit Europe was gaining momentum; technological advances made communication ever easier, distances less off-putting.

Having got the go-ahead in principle from the governors, I had to find a suitable location. Adrian Richardson, headmaster of Cothill, whose 'annexe' at Sauveterre had quickly established itself as a successful and worthwhile project, was extremely helpful. Applications for places at Downe House School continued to increase, so we decided to aim to be operational by September 1991. Finding the right place at the right price within a short time was a challenge. Many kind people, including Patricia Hawkes, a Downe House Old Senior who runs a property business from a lovely château in Burgundy, showed me possible premises. I covered many kilometres and inspected countless 'possibilities', but none was suitable. They all turned out to be too small, or big enough to house the whole school with room to spare for expansion, or too dilapidated, too grand, too remote, too expensive to maintain, too smart to convert for school use, too dreary . . . There were châteaux, gîtes, hunting lodges, *colonies de vacances*, remand homes, old people's homes, and so on. Eventually, I found a little manoir with space for development in a lovely setting close to a small town. We measured and costed, but took too long: we were gazumped at the eleventh hour. Disaster!

The search continued, and one April day, returning from viewing another unworkable 'possibility', I happened upon a signpost to L'Ecole Hampshire in Veyrines-de-Domme. Knowing a bit about Jane Box-Grainger's school, I decided to have a snoop. Jane happened to be there, was most welcoming, showed me round, and gave me a brief resumé of the school's history. Here was a ready-made, officially registered, equipped and staffed school. It was tucked away in a sleepy hamlet, consisting of a few houses, hens, ducks, walnut trees and farms.

After Jane met the governors, we decided that Veyrines should be the French base for Downe House School, and so we went to Veyrines for the first time in September 1991. At first, when Downe House School had exclusive use, they found that the timetable based on the main school timetable was too rigid. It made certain activities impossible. So, gradually, term by term, the timetable was altered and improved. The majority of the lessons were conducted in French and the girls would attempt to converse in French at mealtimes, especially when a member of the Downe House staff sat at table. The charm of the school, with its pretty buildings set round a central courtyard, in a quiet rural location, gave it a homely, secure feel – not too 'schooly'.

Sport and visits continued as before, but the girls needed to get out more. So it was that the '*sortie*' was established as part of the Downe House curriculum in France.

After the examinations at the end of the summer term in 1996, the Lower Sixth A-level group went out to Veyrines. The girls were thinking it would be an escape to the sun; the staff were planning intensive immersion in French. For the first time, Veyrines welcomed back girls who had spent a term there as Lower Fourths. They reminisced and then became very enthusiastic about improving their French, following the 'only French to be spoken' rule and accepting forfeits such as conjugating *spontex* if heard lapsing into English when clearing the tables. They went on '*sorties*', of course. They worked enthusiastically and enjoyed going to Sarlat, Domme and other old haunts. The staff enjoyed these trips too, now that the girls were more independent and mature young people.

So the French visits continue to be a unique aspect of the total Downe House experience. There were early fears that the absence of a pupil from the main school for a whole term would have a detrimental effect on her general progress, but this has been shown to be groundless. Visiting parents were always thrilled by the confidence with which their daughters chattered in French, ordered meals with great aplomb, and showed them sights with pride. After their return, many commented upon their obviously enhanced independent spirits. Perhaps the best testimonials came from the girls themselves. Few returned saying they hadn't enjoyed it, and the reminiscences of the bells and smells of Veyrines and its surroundings were very positive.

I was inspired by Goethe's words:

Concerning all acts of initiative (and creation), there is one elementary truth (the ignorance of which kills countless ideas and splendid plans), that the moment one definitely commits oneself then Providence moves too. All sorts of things occur to help one that would not otherwise have occurred.

Louise Lameret has also made a large contribution to the success of the school. She looks back fondly over many happy years at Veyrines:

In May 1995, I arrived from the school of over a thousand pupils in Cheltenham, to spend a term in a sleepy hamlet lost in the hills of Périgord. I turned up in total blackness, power cuts being a frequent challenge at that time. Jenny Howard, who had by then been in charge of the project for a matter of weeks, gave me a guided tour by torchlight. It was just possible to make out a cosy set of buildings set around a small courtyard, beautifully restored in the local style. I was greeted with a cheerful *"Bonsoir"* from the small community of girls, the atmosphere much more that of a large family home than a school. No noisy, bustling corridors, no lesson bells . . . bliss!

First, supper in the dining room, served by a cheerful Colette: tablecloths and a five-course supper, food brought to the table, girls helping to clear at the end of the meal. Typical school dinners it was not! But, then, Veyrines is unlike any school anywhere else – so much so, that girls seemed to forget they are at school at all. Yes, they have a full academic curriculum, yes their French makes phenomenal progress, but everything is presented in such a way that lessons often do not feel like work.

From the moment they arrive, girls are encouraged to use as much French as possible, be it on a *'sortie'* to a local school, over lunch with friends and staff, or – in the days before risk assessment – during a weekend spent with a French family. What an experience that was! I wish I could remember the name of the girl who spent her weekend with the family of a local sculptor. They had made their home in a cave with the most spectacular views over the valley, no way primitive, as one might imagine, but even the bathtub had been hewn from the rock!

In those days, before the 35-hour week and HACCP (a draconian system of food hygiene regulations), the school ran on what now seems like a skeleton staff. Georges, the chef, prepared wonderful meals; Colette served and kept the school looking spick and span; Mike Roberts did the books; and Pascale Lavarello and Marie-Christine Nicholas, along with Jenny and myself, did all the teaching. Two *surveillantes,* Lindsay and Vicki, looked after the dormitories and organised activities for the girls. Zizu the cat, and Roxanne the collie dog, also seemed like part of the team. Roxanne liked to join in games of rounders in the square, and Zizu had her kittens in the staffroom!

Then, as now, girls saw the term as the most special of their school careers. An enormous amount was squeezed into the short time spent with us. In addition to the regular timetable of lessons and '*sorties*', they had tuition in music, orchestra and dance classes. There was tennis-coaching too at the club in Sarlat, and frequent visits from Madame Pommier, who tried her best to teach us to sing – sometimes in local dialect! Each term culminated in a soirée, when schools were invited to the school to be entertained by the girls and treated to aperitifs to die for, prepared by Georges.

My term's contract was renewed, and though that power cut seems like yesterday, twelve years have flown by. Many staff and many more girls have been and gone. There have been numerous changes, but the heart of the place remains the same. Occasionally, there is a knock at the door and a familiar face says, "*Bonjour, Madame.*" A girl has come back to visit, grown-up and graduated, having never forgotten her term in Veyrines.

The girls visited Futuroscope to study science. Each visit took three days, including an overnight stay and travelling on French trains.

Futuroscope.

Music lessons at Veyrines with Harriet Wagner.

Art lessons associated with Roc de Cazelle.

Pupils outside the church in Veyrines-de-Domme,
Autumn 2006.

Photograph collage: pupils on a gabare *on the River Dordogne; pupils among the poppies near the school; the Château de la Malartrie at La Roque Gageac.*

ON VEYRINES

[*Taken from the school magazine, Summer 2006*]

"*Levez-vous, les filles, levez vous!*" This, in case we have not heard the loud clanging of the church bell at 7.00. "Too early", groans one girl, turning onto her other side for an extra five minutes of sleep. By the time the night staff come round with our laundry at 7.35, we are just about conscious and ready to say "*Bonjour, Madame Dubernat*" in chorus – so at least she thinks we are awake.

Struggling down to breakfast by 7.55 with our laces undone and t-shirts on back to front, we are grateful to sit down and tuck into our 'pain au chocolat', especially if we've managed to avoid one of the clearing places at the tables. As another typical day starts at Veyrines towards the end of a memorable term, we look back over the range of experiences we have lived through.

We remember vividly the day we arrived, when we were both excited and nervous about coming. As soon as we saw the school, surrounded by nothing but fields and trees, we knew this was going to be a special term.

Firstly we were introduced to all the teachers before being shown into our dorms – spacious and each named after different parts of the Périgord Area. We barely had time to unpack before we were ushered down to supper. Wow! – five courses: soup, starter with salad, main course, cheese, dessert. With an activity afterwards (voluntary) to pass the evening away quickly. For those going to Veyrines in the future, we can guarantee you one thing: you will never be bored.

Every day at Veyrines is different. Lessons are fun and unpredictable and last an hour. Seems a long time, but you quickly get used to it. We did not expect that lessons would include making a flower press, or (in English) learning how to solve cryptic crossword clues – even from The Times and the Daily Telegraph!

We learnt a great deal from the "*sorties*" we went on at least twice a week. These were really lessons which took place away from school instead of in a classroom, and took us to all kinds of interesting places in the Dordogne. Beware! You can easily get caught out if you don't pay attention: teachers are likely to spring a pop quiz on you without warning. So make sure you listen to the guide!

"*Tests in Maths, Histoire/Go and VQ today, Girls. Piece of cake as long as you know it all.*" Why test us if they think we know it already?

Whose fault is it we are worn out before we get to the first lesson?? Still, only an hour to survive before break. Then a two hour "*sortie*" and it's lunch. We told you life is tough here. With a French speaker at the head of each lunch table, we can show off how much we have forgotten of what we learnt in *Theorie* two hours earlier. So what? – They mark us not on accuracy, but on willingness to speak – do Downe House guys ever have a problem with that – even in French?

And so, into the afternoon. If we are supposed to be having an introduction to the French way of life, how come they overlook 'la sieste'? Everyone else has a two hour snooze after lunch – why not us?

Do we complain? Or do we press on knowing that supper is only just round the corner? Hoping the timetable might allow us a brief respite in the form of a lesson of EPS – PE to anyone else. There is no sports hall here, no playing field, but the tennis court is very versatile. Throwing a Frisbee about is considered a sporting activity here. The handball game we learnt apparently came originally from Germany. Gymnasts enjoy acrosport – a kind of gymnastics routine performed to noisy music. At least we get to do that in the village hall – '*la salle des fêtes*'.

We have to survive on just five courses at supper – but we manage. After supper, Mme Beese's enthusiasm persuades a lot of us to join in a creative activity of some kind. By the time that finishes, we are all ready for a good old chinwag – and what do they do? They send us to bed! We don't mind the quiet time before lights go out – but how are we supposed to stay quiet after?? There is so much still to talk about! Whispering, so they can't hear you from outside the dorm, just isn't the same.

A "*Sortie*" can take you anywhere from a château, to a cave, to a truffle farm, to a paper making factory, to a walnut museum, to a French school, to the kitchen of a restaurant.

Living like the French really helps you learn more about the difference in culture: not just the language, but paying with Euros, sports that French children enjoy, such as disco-golf and handball, a strawberry fair with a strawberry tart several metres long, a Saturday evening village fair where everyone ate at tables in the car park!

We won't tell you too much about other things like water parks, rides on a *gabare*, flying between trees at an air park – you'll find out soon enough when your parents come to take you out. And Futuroscope is just so different. Quite a long journey, but well worth it, and a night away in a nice hotel.

On Sunday, we attended Mass at the abbey in St Cyprien. Interesting to see how this differs from our services at home. We noticed that there were a lot more people in the market than in the church!

We all wonder at the beginning of term how we are going to cope listening to French all day – and especially having to speak French with the teachers at lunch. If lunch is quiet at the start of term, it certainly isn't by the time we leave/ Hooray! We do not have to take any exams – but we have endless tests. Why do the French use so much vocabulary??

In summary, we have had a wonderful term in a calm, peaceful region of France. Teachers have been so patient and helpful. Everyone has been so friendly. Yes, we have had a lot of fun, but we have learned an enormous amount as well.

Au Revoir, Veyrines. We shall miss you.

Contributions from Alexandra Ames, Samantha Lui, Iona Gordon Lennox, Alexia Peel Yates, Harriet Green, Francesca Whitehead, Stephanie Green, Charlotte Wyatt – Lower IV.

Picture of 'Presse Fleurs'.

Picture of 'Presse Fleurs'.

In the kitchen.

Domme.

A visit to the school.

What do the girls themselves think of the Veyrines Experience? Here is a selection of quotes:

- What is there to say? I loved every minute.

- An experience I will never forget.

- It's so busy we hardly have any time to rest – too busy to be homesick.

- At first I was nervous, but now I realise it is a wonderful experience and everyone should make the most of it.

- I thought that speaking French at lunch would be horrible, but it just made me more confident.

- In culture and Vie Quotidienne, we have learnt the French way of life and their habits.

- The "Sorties" have been a great way to learn everything – it was good to see so much of the Dordogne.

- I hope when I'm older I can flick through my "journal" and remember my term there.

- The teachers are really helpful when I find French hard to understand: I never feel too embarrassed to make a mistake speaking to them.

- The children at the primary school were sweet and enthusiastic – it was interesting to visit their actual school.

- Meeting people in the street is sometimes scary, but talking to children is brilliant.

- The meals are luxury – it is so civilised being served at table.

- The activities were brilliant – a great way to spend the evenings.

- I liked the freedom of going on walks when you want – French people normally talk and wave to me, which is nice.

- Futuroscope was really good – I learnt how much science has developed and is still developing.

- Tests may be necessary but they aren't great fun!

- Even though I want to go home, I wish I were coming back next term; it feels strange that someone else will be sleeping in my bed!

OUTINGS

The chapel at Montferrand.

The insect museum.

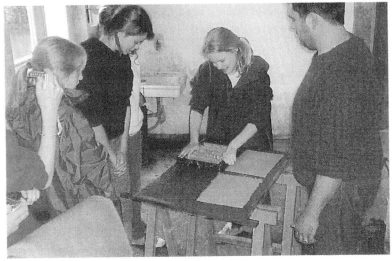

Papermaking at Couze.

When I visited the school in 2007 I met Eric and Vie Reynolds. They were in charge of the school at that time. They impressed me with their enthusiasm for our project.

With the changing times, a new fire escape had to be constructed for the upper floors of the *grange*. Artistically it was a difficult task to prevent the new structure from spoiling the beautiful Périgordin architecture and to leave the maximum space for the small garden. I am very pleased with the result, but I wonder if the fire escape was really necessary. The school, after all, had managed successfully since 1981 without it!

In 2007 Eric adapted two famous French playwright's works for the pupils to perform at the end of the summer term – an exciting and stimulating way to study the language. Overleaf can be seen the programme and cast list for Jean Anouilh's *Humulus le Muet* and Molière's *Tartuffe*. The plays were performed in Domme on 9 June 2007 – an imaginative way to integrate the pupils into the locality.

I was sad to hear that Eric and Vie were returning to England owing to family problems. I wish them the very best for a happy future.

Les élèves de l'Ecole Downe House à Veyrines de Domme

présentent

HUMULUS LE MUET

de Jean Anouilh
Version adaptée
suivi de

TARTUFFE

de Molière
Interprétation abrégée en anglais

Salle de la Rode
Domme
Samedi 9 juin 2007
18h00

Programme front cover.

HUMULUS LE MUET

La Duchesse, Grand-mère d'Humulus	(Henrietta Nicholson
	(Eleanor Manners
Hector de Brignoc	Rebecca Speare-Cole
Humulus enfant	Georgia Walton
Humulus adolescent	Lucia Saint Clair-Erskine
Le Gouverneur	(Alexandra Cohen
	(Sophia MacKay
Hélène	Hermione Corfield
Yvette, la bonne	Catherine Brown
Gaston, le jardinier	Hebe Cockcroft
Estelle, la femme de ménage	Pandora Monnas
Hippolyte, l'entraîneur personnel	Chloe Searle

Narrateurs :
Lukyn Gedge
Alexa Coleridge Cole
Saskia von Stumm
Emily Comyn

Metteurs en scène:
Hélène Bougot
Eric Reynolds

Acte 1
Chez Madame la Duchesse

Acte 2
Chez Madame la Duchesse, 10 ans plus tard

Acte 3
A la campagne

TARTUFFE

Orgon   Lukyn Gedge, Chloe Searle
Le personnage principal qui est sous l'influence de l'hypocrite Tartuffe

Elmire   Hebe Cockcroft, Lucia Saint Clair-Erskine
La femme d'Orgon qui montre une attitude raisonnable envers la vie

Damis   Camilla Beazley
Le fils d'Orgon qui essaie de prouver que Tartuffe est un hypocrite et qui ne réussit qu'à se faire déshériter

Mariane   Alexa Coleridge Cole, Sophia MacKay
La fille d'Orgon qui est amoureuse de Valère et qui est forcée de se marier avec Tartuffe

Madame Pernelle   Henrietta Nicholson
La mère d'Orgon qui est totalement dupée par Tartuffe

Valère   Eleanor Manners, Catherine Brown
Le soupirant de Mariane qui est rejeté par Orgon en faveur de Tartuffe

Cléante   Saskia von Stumm
Le beau-frère d'Orgon qui essaie d'obtenir de chacun qu'il considère les choses avec calme et raison

Tartuffe   Alexandra Cohen, Rebecca Speare-Cole
Le religieux hypocrite qui se débrouille à gagner la confiance d'Orgon et qui ensuite le trahit

Dorine   Hermione Corfield, Georgia Walton
La servante de Mariane qui est également une manipulatrice et commentatrice rusée des actions de la pièce

Flipote   Emily Comyn
La servante de Mme Pernelle

Monsieur Loyal   Pandora Monnas
L'agent de police qui s'occupe des papiers d'expulsion d'Orgon

Narrateurs :
Camilla Beazley, Henrietta Nicholson, Emily Comyn, Pandora Monnas
Saskia von Stumm

Metteur en scène : Dee Pomson

Toute l'action a lieu dans la maison d'Orgon

La pièce raconte l'histoire d'un homme diabolique et d'un homme stupide. L'homme diabolique s'appelle Tartuffe qui, en mentant et en agissant, fait croire à l'homme plutôt stupide qui s'appelle Orgon qu'il est bon! Orgon l'a invité à vivre chez lui et a ordonné à toute sa famille de le respecter. Seule la mère d'Orgon, Mme Pernelle, pense que Tartuffe est vraiment bon. Le reste de la famille sait qu'il les dupe et ils refusent d'être gentils!

Cast list.

99

Eric and Vie with a group of girls.

After a visit to the boulangerie.

Hot chocolate in the garden before going to bed.

The following information was sent to parents before their daughters spent a term in Veyrines:

VEYRINES: A VERY SPECIAL TERM IN FRANCE
BY ALISON GWATKIN

'La France Profonde'

Winding through the beautiful valley of the Dordogne, hillsides clothed in ancient châteaux, clusters of creamy yellow houses clinging to the cobbled streets, backing in glorious golden light, sums up the road to our French house in Veyrines. In summer, the fields and hedgerows are strewn with wild flowers and the scent hangs in the air. The descent into the village square of this sleepy hamlet, overflowing with geranium laden window boxes, it's famous telephone box – symbol of contact with England before the advent of mobile telephones – is dominated by the sights and sounds of about twenty of our teenage girls chattering like magpies in French, in English, in a mixture of both. To this idyllic setting, Downe has become the life and soul of the party!

A Unique Experience

The school is led by Eric Reynolds and his wife Vie. Eric is ably supported by Louise Lameret, who has become a bit of an institution over the years! They are supported in turn by a loyal and enthusiastic French team, who enjoy sharing this unique French experience with the girls. The focus of life is the 'sortie', where the girls go out in small groups to practise their French in real, live situations. There is no limit to the scope and imagination engaged in these activities, whether it is truffle hunting, jewellery making, shopping at the local market, or visiting a local Château, once the home of Josephine Baker, and now home to a fabulous falconry centre. Our girls were featured in the publicity brochure on one of their visits.

At school, French is made accessible to everyone, not just those naturally good at languages. This was the aim of the project at the outset. Speaking French is fun, and lunchtime conversation in French carries a mark like no other exercise. The whole experience is to embrace everyone, instilling self confidence in a smaller boarding community – and this it has done, looking back with the help of their journals on a very special term in their school life.

Part of the Community!

Over the years, more and more links with the local community have been forged. Now, concerts and plays performed at the Old People's Home, local primary schools, or in the *Mairie* across the road, demonstrate the wealth of artistic talent at Downe, which girls are always willing to share. One of the highlights of the year takes place in the Michaelmas Term, with the rest of France in a Charity Event called Telethon, the equivalent of our 'Children In Need' Campaign. Large sums are raised and we take the stage in a local theatre for the evening, thanks to the influence of Hervé, the husband of one of our staff, Sylvie. She started her Downe House life as the Assistant here in England, before moving on to be Assistant Housemistress to Hermitage, and then home to France to work in Veyrines. She is one of our longest serving members of staff, along with Vicky Besse, who helps the girls to feel at home.

Each term ends with a grand finale, when a formal dinner takes place with invited guests, and the *'Maire',* who presents the certificates and prizes at the end of the candlelit meal and entertainment. The achievement of each individual is recognised and the girls return to Downe confident of their success.

I wish Alison Gwatkin a happy and successful time in Veyrines.

Visit to l'ecole primaire.

Visit to the old people's home.

Spring 2006 – changing seasons.

Pupils enjoying an unusual snowfall.

Summer 2006 – the new fire escape is seen (just) behind the wisteria!

After Mass at the Abbey of St Cyprien.

In the River Céou.

Summer 2006.

Chapter 14

Epilogue

In May 2007, I returned to look at the school which I had founded in 1977, thirty years before. I was in the process of writing this chronicle, and I wanted to see for myself how the school was faring. On arrival at the school, I was greeted most warmly by Eric and Vie Reynolds, who had been running the school for Downe House for four years.

It gave me great pleasure to see the school operating so successfully, and to be the recipient, as founder, of so many kind words and compliments.

I enjoyed renewing acquaintances with Colette and Louise as well as the *maire*, Francis Vierge, who was only a councillor in my years between 1977 and 1993. Monsieur Vierge reminded me that his daughter had been a 'holiday pupil' at the school.

Looking back at my notes of the description of Veyrines before I decided to purchase the farmhouse, I can see I describe the village as a 'little hamlet in the heart of Périgord Noir, typical of the region and that period'. There were 198 inhabitants and 1,440 hectares of cultivated land, fields and woods. The *ecole primaire* looked down on Veyrines, its boundaries all wooded, so typical of the region.

In 1977, we asked some locals in St Cyprien if they had heard of Veyrines-de-Domme. Mostly they replied, "*Je ne le connais pas*" or "*Peut-être c'est près de Bordeaux*" (130 kilometres away!). Some suggested that perhaps it was near Bergerac. (An hour's drive from Veyrines!) So in 1977 I thought it safe to conclude that the hamlet was unknown to many people – even among the locals!

Back to 2007: It gave me great pleasure to see the school's pre-revolutionary buildings in such excellent shape, and to see that they had still retained their original Périgordin charm.

I feel, and felt, both humbled and overwhelmed to find this educational project had proven such a huge success!

I want to thank The Hampshire School and all the schools and groups who visited us, not forgetting the individuals and family pupils who supported the school. Downe House makes a great contribution. I enjoy meeting, here in London and in other places, parents and grandparents whose daughters attend or have attended the school, and they tell me how much they have enjoyed learning in this original and unique way.

On the administrative front, I have to thank my accountant, Robert Berthomier of Sarlat, for his help and guidance over the last twenty-five years. On the legal front, David Goodchild's help has been invaluable. David was a non-executive director of my husband's firm, Telephone Rentals plc, as well as being a director of Clifford Chance in Paris. I am also grateful to my son Paul, managing director of Hampshire Tutorials Ltd, who brokered the sale of L'Ecole Hampshire to Downe House magnificently.

I thank everyone who has contributed to the school, and made it a hub of activity in a tiny hamlet in the Dordogne, and a wonderful educational experience. Everyone knows it now – in France as well as in England.

Veyrines-de-Domme in 1981.
The ecole primaire was closed some years ago, and is now used as rented flats.

HOTEL
LE PERIGORD
Le Port de Domme
24250 La Roque Gageac

*Madame Jane Box-Grainger
à le plaisir et l'honneur d'inviter les membres
des Ecoles Hampshire et Downe house
à un dîner anniversaire*

Mardi 31 Août 1993 (Réception à 17 heures)

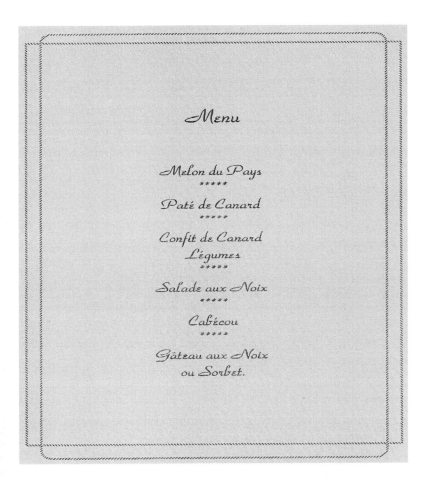

Menu

Melon du Pays
*****

Paté de Canard
*****

Confit de Canard
Légumes
*****

Salade aux Noix
*****

Cabécou
*****

Gâteau aux Noix
ou Sorbet.

The menu to say goodbye to my staff and to give exclusive use of L'Ecole Hampshire to Downe House from September 1993. The meal was typically Périgordian and de la région.

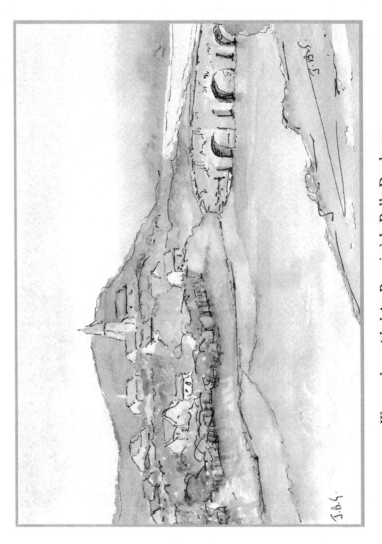

Watercolour titled Au Revoir à la Belle Dordogne.

Appendix I

Cultural Visits

When starting visits, proximity to the school had to be taken into account so that pupils would be able to spend the maximum time exploring the venue, instead of travelling to and from it. The school is very fortunate in that it is well situated for many excellent visits.

I have included here some of the most popular attractions. Each will be described briefly for readers who are unfamiliar with our area.

THE CHATEAU DE CASTELNAUD

About twenty minutes from Veyrines is the historic Château de Castelnaud on the south side of the River Dordogne.

Travelling south from the school, we get our first glimpse of the château in the distance.

Watercolour of the château with poppies in the foreground.

The bridge over the Dordogne connecting Beynac to the village.

We pass en route a typical small building of the region called a *borie*. This was used as a shepherd's hut in the past. The roof is constructed of *lauzes* – the flat limestone tiles typical of this region.

Watercolour of the borie.

Castelnaud-la-Chapelle on the south side of the river faces Beynac on the north. Both villages are crowned by picturesque and dramatic châteaux. The owners of the châteaux were rivals since the twelfth century. The Cazenac family owned Castelnaud and supported the English in the Wars of the Middle Ages, while the owners of Beynac supported the French.

The pupils enjoyed visiting the Château de Castelnaud with its lovely views over the Dordogne and surrounding countryside.

Florent Tuelé's drawing of the château.

I wonder what has happened to this brilliant young cartoonist?
This is Edward Petrie's view of his visit to the Château de Castelnaud.

THE CHATEAU DE BEYNAC

The château overlooking the River Dordogne.

This Château is about half an hour's drive from the school.

The origins of this château are not medieval, despite its appearance. Bronze Age people occupied the site during the ninth and tenth centuries in order to control the valley. Then came the Gauls, who wanted to control trade on the river. But the castle itself actually dates from the twelfth century. Its square tower was doubtless designed to overlook the river when the Viking longboats reached this far up, sowing terror everywhere throughout the region. Later Beynac became one of the four Baronies of Périgord, resisting all attempts to capture it, until Richard Coeur de Lion and Simon de Montfort finally succeeded.

The village of Beynac is a delight to visit. One can wander through its ancient little streets, passing the tiny squares on your way to the castle, then going on upwards to the medieval chapel and the wonderful panorama over the valley. Like the artist Pissarro, the poet Éluard, and the author Henry Miller, you may also admire it and think it is worth staying there.

The pupils enjoyed this visit very much.

Le Château de Beynac

H. Gwyther's pencil sketch of the Château de Beynac.

A nine-year-old's impression of the Château de Beynac.

A group from The Hampshire School on the ramparts of the château.

A flat-bottomed boat called a gabare *on the river below the château. In the past* gabares *were used for transporting wine and other goods up the river. Today they are used for pleasure trips in the summer months.*

DOMME

Another very popular visit was to the French bastide of Domme. It is perched on a promontory overlooking one of the loveliest parts of the Dordogne Valley. The bastide was fortified against the English during the wars of the Middle Ages. It is surrounded by walls known as *remparts* through which you could enter by three fortified gates called the Porte des Tours, the Porte de la Combe and the Porte del Bos. The pupils enjoyed visiting this ancient bastide with its little streets and colourful tourist shops and the panoramic view of the Dordogne.

In 1307 the Porte des Tours became a prison for the Knights Templars. The Templars were a religious and military order founded to protect the pilgrims en route to the Holy Land. They became very rich landowners and they were accused of lending money at extortionate rates of interest. Philip IV, King of France, was angry at the Templars' activities and had more than 5,000 French Templars arrested. They were persecuted and tortured to obtain confessions of guilt.

In 1970 the late Chanoine P. M. Tonnellier analysed the graffiti in the Porte des Tours. He believed that the Templars were almost certainly innocent. Their sad drawings and pleas of 'Save us' can still be seen today in the Porte des Tours. They remain a heartbreaking piece of visual history.

In this limestone area there are many wonderful caves to visit. Domme possesses the largest natural caves of the Périgord Noir. A cave situated beneath the seventeenth-century town hall was used as a shelter in World War II, but today many visitors go there to see the stalactites and stalagmites, which have been floodlit artistically. Some students really enjoyed this part of their visit to Domme.

Watercolour titled View of the Dordogne from Les Remparts.

Pen and wash of the Porte des Tours.

Watercolour of the largest natural cave in the Périgord Noir.

A group of pupils shopping in Domme.

SARLAT

Sarlat was the home of the poet Étienne de la Boétie and is one of the most beautiful towns in the area. Its fine architecture is admired by its many visitors.

Sarlat was built during the Middle Ages on the site of a monastery where today you can see the Cathedral of St Sacerdos. There still exist some twelfth-century houses, which are inhabited. Most of the *hôtels-des-particuliers* (private mansions) were built between the fifteenth and sixteenth centuries. The Hôtel de Maleville and the Hôtel de Plamon are the most famous. Outside the cathedral there are typical French markets held twice a week. All around the square there are cafés where one can sit outside and admire the beautiful architecture. The visit to Sarlat was enjoyed by all ages, including the visiting monitors and supervisors. As a special treat on Saturday evenings after supper, all pupils of fourteen years and older were allowed to revisit the town to admire the architecture by night, and they were permitted *un verre de vin.*

The house where Étienne de la Boétie lived.

St Cyprien

Each Sunday we went to St Cyprien, a medieval city full of picturesque little streets. It is built in an old amphitheatre on the slope of the hillside near the River Dordogne. The city extends around an ancient abbey in an undulating wooded valley. St Cyprien is about twenty minutes' drive from the school.

Some pupils and teachers went to church in the abbey. Then we would all look around the little market stalls which filled the whole of the main street. The pupils and staff enjoyed the relaxed and typically French atmosphere, as well as another opportunity to shop for French delicacies. Among their purchases some pupils were attracted to buy bottles of wine (ostensibly for their parents) whilst others purchased knives. Both alcohol and knives were handed in on return to the school and locked in their suitcases, so that their parents would receive their gifts on their return home, and the knives would cause no damage when being brandished about.

Watercolour of the Abbey of St Cyprien.

The Dordogne and Vézère region is not only renowned for its scenic and architectural beauty; it also claims to be the Capital of Prehistory. In the valley of the Vézère particularly there are many caves, and evidence of prehistoric man and animals can be seen. Lascaux is one of the most well-known caves with drawings of prehistoric man and animals. When it was first opened the fresh air and the breath of the sightseers caused the drawings to deteriorate; so Lascaux II, an exact replica of the first cave, was constructed and the original cave was closed except for special visitors.

My experience was that not many of the young pupils enjoyed visiting the caves and their drawings. Font de Gaume was an exception because it has the most splendid and dramatic drawings of animals, including horses, bison, oxen, deer, mammoths, ibexes and bears. Also at La Roque St Christophe the pupils enjoyed visiting the dwellings of troglodytic inhabitants and the magnificent staircase, hewn out of the cliffs, which leads up to the cave.

The prehistoric sites of Périgord.

129

Appendix II

Views of the Farm Domaine in 1977

The farmhouse from the village square.

The bakehouse from the chemin rural.

The grange, *and the courtyard filled with nettles and branches.*

The pigsty, difficult to see behind the bakehouse and overgrown vegetation.

The farmhouse from the chemin rural.

The grange *from the village square.*

Appendix III

The Front Cover of the School Prospectus

This prospectus was sent to schools and other prospective clients.

Signatures

Signatures

Signatures